钱这东西

Money Talks

李溪 编译

外文出版社

图书在版编目（CIP）数据

钱这东西/李湲编译．—北京：外文出版社，2005（笑话集锦）
ISBN 7-119-04250-5

Ⅰ.钱... Ⅱ.李... Ⅲ.英语-对照读物，笑话-英、汉
Ⅳ.H319.4：Ⅰ

中国版本图书馆 CIP 数据核字（2005）第 111246 号

外文出版社网址：
　http://www.flp.com.cn
外文出版社电子信箱：
　info@flp.com.cn
　sales@flp.com.cn

笑话集锦
钱这东西

编　　译　李　湲
责任编辑　李春英
封面设计　李迎迎
印刷监制　冯　浩
出版发行　外文出版社
社　　址　北京市百万庄大街 24 号　　　邮政编码　100037
电　　话　（010）68995883（编辑部）
　　　　　（010）68329514/68327211（推广发行部）
印　　刷　三河市汇鑫印务有限公司
经　　销　新华书店/外文书店
开　　本　32 开　　　　　　　　　字　　数　30 千字
印　　数　5001—10000 册　　　　　印　　张　6
版　　次　2006 年第 1 版第 2 次印刷
装　　别　平
书　　号　ISBN 7-119-04250-5
定　　价　9.8 元

目 录
Contents

If you owe the bank $100,
that's your problem.

If you owe the bank $100
million, that's the bank's problem.

如果你欠银行 100 块钱，
那是你的问题。

如果你欠银行 100 万，那
就是银行的问题了。

Parking Fee

An Indian walks into a New York City bank and asks to see the loan officer. He says he is going to Europe on business for two weeks and needs to borrow $5,000.

The bank officer says the bank will need some kind of security for such a loan, so the man hand over the keys of a new Rolls Royce parked on the street in front of the bank.

Everything is checked out, and the bank agrees to accept the car as collateral for the loan.

An employee drives the Rolls into the bank's underground garage and parks it there.

停车费

一个印度人走进纽约城市银行要见贷款客户服务经理。他说他要去欧洲出差两个星期，因此要借贷 5 000 美元。

客服经理说银行规定这样的借贷需要有担保，于是这人递上停在银行外街边的一辆劳斯莱斯新车的钥匙。

里里外外捡查了一遍之后，银行同意用他的车作担保。

一个职员把这辆劳斯莱斯开进了银行的地库存放。

Two weeks later, the man returns, repays the $5,000 and the interest, which comes to $15.41.

The loan officer says, "We are very happy to have had your business, and this transaction has worked out very nicely, but we are a little puzzled. While you were away, we checked you out and found that you are a multimillionaire. What puzzles us is why would you bother to borrow $5,000?"

The Indian replied, "Where else in New York can I park my car for two weeks for 15 bucks?"

两个星期后，印度人回来了，还清了 5 000 元和 15.41 元的利息。

贷款客服经理说："我们银行很高兴能有你做主顾，我们之间的这笔业务已经圆满完成了。只是我们还有一点儿困惑。你不在的这段时间里，我们核实了你的情况，发现你是个千万富翁。让我们不能理解的是你为什么要来借区区 5 000 元？"

印度人答道："纽约还有什么地方能让我只花15 块钱就把我这辆车存两个星期呢？"

☆ collateral /kɒˈlætərəl/ *n.* 担保品

My Mother

I was walking through the supermarket to pick up a few things when I noticed an old lady following me around. Thinking nothing of it, I ignored her and continued on.

Finally I went to the checkout line, but she got in front of me.

"Pardon me," she said, "I'm sorry if my staring at you has made you feel uncomfortable. It's just that you look just like my son, who just died recently."

"I'm very sorry," I said to her, "Is there anything I can do for you?"

"Yes," she said, "As I'm leaving, can you say 'Goodbye, Mother'? It would make me feel so much better."

我妈妈

我在超市里转悠着想要买些东西，可我注意到一个老太太总是跟着我。不过我觉得这没什么，就不理她，继续转。

最后，我到付款台排队时，她赶到了我前面。

"打扰一下，"她说，"我很抱歉，我盯着你看，看得你很不舒服。我这样做只是因为你长得太像我儿子了，他刚刚去世了。"

"我很难过，"我说，"我能为你做什么吗？"

"是的，"她说，"我走的时候，你能对我说一声'妈妈，再见'吗？这会使我心里好过些的。"

"Sure," I said. An odd request, but no harm would come of it.

As the old woman was leaving, I called out, "Goodbye, Mother!"

As I stepped up to the checkout counter, I saw that my total was $257.50.

"How can that be?" I asked, "I only purchased a few things!"

"Your mother said that you would pay for her," said the clerk.

"当然，"我说。这虽然是个奇怪的要求，可对我来说也没什么损失。

老太太要走的时候，我大声说："妈妈，再见！"

等我到付款台前，我发现我的账单是257.5元。

"这怎么可能?"我问道，"我没买多少东西呀！"

"你妈妈说你会为她付账的，"收银员说。

钱 这 东 西

I Didn't Get Any Money
This Time

A man in a bar sees a friend at a table, drinking by himself.

Approaching the friend he comments, "You look terrible. What's the problem?"

"My mother died in November," he said, "and left me $50,000."

"Gee, that's tough," he replied.

"Then in December," the friend continued, "My father died, leaving me $98,000."

"Wow. Two parents gone in two months. No wonder you're depressed."

我这次没钱了

一个人去酒吧，看到一个朋友独自一人坐在桌旁喝酒。

他走上前去，问道："你看上去很不好，出什么事了？"

"11月我妈妈去世了，"他的朋友答道，"留给我5万块钱。"

"哎呀，太不幸了。"

"跟着12月我的父亲又去世了，留给我9万8千块钱。"

"天哪，双亲在两个月内相继去世，难怪你这么消沉。"

"And last month my aunt died, and left me $20,000."

"Three close family members lost in three months? How sad."

"Then this month," continued the friend, "absolutely nothing!"

"上个月我姑姑去世了，留给我两万块钱。"

"三个月里失去三位近亲？这太令人伤心了。"

"可是这个月，"他的朋友接着说道，"什么也没有了。"

I Want to Take Money with Me

As Mr. Smith was on his death bed, he attempted to formulate a plan that would allow him to take at least some of his wealth with him.

He called for the three men he trusted most — his lawyer, his doctor, and his clergyman.

He told them, "I'm going to give you each $30,000 in cash before I die. At my funeral, I want you to place the money in my coffin so that I can try to take it with me."

All three agreed to do this and were given the money. At the funeral, each approached the coffin in turn and placed an envelope inside.

我想带走我的钱

史密斯先生快要死了，他想到一个计划能让他在死后带走至少一部分财产。

他叫来自己最信任的三个人——他的律师、私人医生和牧师。

他对他们说："我死前会给你们每人 3 万块钱，我要你们在我的葬礼上把这些钱放到我的棺材里，这样我才好尽量把它们带走。"

那三个人都同意这样做并拿到了钱。葬礼上，三个人依次走到棺材前，然后把一个信封放进去。

While leaving the cemetery, the clergyman said, "I have to confess something to you fellows. Brother Smith was a good churchman all his life, and I know he would have wanted me to do this. The church needed a new baptistery very badly, and I took $10,000 of the money he gave me and bought one. I only put $20,000 in the coffin."

The physician then said, "Well, since we're confiding in one another, I might as well tell you that I didn't put the full $30,000 in the coffin either. Smith had a disease that could have been diagnosed sooner if I had this very new machine, but the machine cost $20,000 and I couldn't afford it then. I used $20,000 of the

从墓地离开时，牧师说道："我有事情要对你们忏悔。教友史密斯终身都是虔诚的教徒，我相信他会要我这样做的。教堂里急需一个新的浸礼池，我就从他给我的钱里拿出 1 万块买了一个，所以我只在他的棺材里放了 2 万块钱。"

医生跟着说道："既然我们互相信任，那么我得告诉你们我也没有把那 3 万块钱都放进棺材里。史密斯先生得了一种病，如果我有一种最先进的仪器的话就能早些诊断出来，可是那仪器要 2 万块钱，当时我买不起。所以我从那笔钱里拿出 2 万块

money to buy the machine so that I might be able to save another patient. I know that Smith would have wanted me to do that."

The lawyer then said, "I'm ashamed of both of you. When I put my envelope into that coffin, it held my personal check for the full $30,000."

买了仪器，这样我就能用它救治其他的病人。我想
史密斯先生会让我这样做的。"

律师接着说："我真替你们两个害臊。我放进
棺材的那个信封里可是有一张我签的整整 3 万元的
个人支票。"

☆ **baptistery** /ˈbæptɪstəri/ *n.*【宗】洗礼堂；浸礼池

钱 这 东 西

Bankrupt

Broke, a bank closed its doors to shut out a rush of its depositors.

One man stood in front of the large glass doors and yelled for all to hear, "They ought to throw the bank president in jail. They ought to take the whole board of trustees and hang them from the nearest tree. Every person who works in the bank should be tarred and feathered and run out of town!"

A policeman asks, "Is your money in that bank?"

The man says, "If I had money in that bank, would I be taking it this lightly?"

破 产

一家银行破产了，不得不关上大门以阻挡蜂拥而来的储户们。

一个人站在银行巨大的玻璃门前，大声叫着，好让所有人都听到。"他们该把这家银行的总裁关进监狱。他们该把所有董事会的人抓起来，把他们挂在最近的树上。这家银行的所有职员都该被涂上柏油、粘上羽毛，然后赶出城去！"

一个警察问他："你有钱存在这家银行？"

那人说："要是我有钱在这儿，我哪能就这么认啦？"

☆ **tar and feather** 把（人）浑身涂满柏油并粘上羽毛（一种私刑或侮辱）；严惩

21

钱 这 东 西

How Could You Do This

A blonde was down on her luck. In order to raise some money, she decided to kidnap a kid and hold him for ransom.

She went to the playground, grabbed a little boy, took him behind a tree, and told him, "I've kidnapped you."

She then wrote a note saying, "I've kidnapped your kid. Tomorrow morning, put $10,000 in a paper bag and put it under the pecan tree next to the slide on the north side of the playground. Signed, A Blonde."

The blonde pinned the note to the kid's shirt and sent him home to show it to his parents.

你怎么能这么做

一个金发女郎正值背运。为了弄到些钱花，她决定绑架一个小孩索取赎金。

于是她去了游乐园，抓起一个小男孩，带到一棵树后，对他说："我绑架了你。"

然后，她写了一张条子："我绑架了你的小孩。明天早上，用纸袋装 10 000 块钱放在游乐园北侧儿童滑梯旁边的山核桃树下。——一个金发女郎。"

她把纸条别在小男孩的衬衣上后就把他送回家给他父母看。

The next morning the blonde checked, and sure enough, a paper bag was sitting beneath the pecan tree. The blonde opened up the bag and found the $10,000 with a note that said, "How could you do this to a fellow blonde?"

第二天早上，金发女郎去树下查看，那里果然有一个纸袋。打开纸袋，里面有 10 000 块钱和一张纸条，上面写着："你怎么能对另一个金发女郎做这样的事呢？"

☆ **ransom** /ˈrænsəm/ *n.* 赎金

☆ **pecan** /pɪˈkæn/ *n.* 美洲山核桃树

钱 这 东 西

The Best Time

A prisoner in jail receives a letter from his wife: "Dear Husband, I have decided to plant some lettuce in the back garden. When is the best time to plant them?"

The prisoner, knowing that the prison guards read all mail, replied in a letter: "Dear Wife, whatever you do, do not touch the back garden. That is where I hid all the money."

A week or so later, he received another letter from his wife: "Dear Husband, You wouldn't believe what happened, some men came with shovels to the house, and dug up all the back garden."

The prisoner wrote another letter back: "Dear Wife, now is the best time to plant the lettuce."

最佳时机

监狱里的一个犯人收到了妻子的一封信："亲爱的老公，我准备在后院里种些生菜，什么时候下种最好呢？"

这个犯人知道狱警们会检查所有的来往信件，于是在回信中写道："亲爱的老婆，不管你做什么都不要动后院，因为我把所有的钱都藏在那儿了。"

大约一个星期之后，他又收到妻子的来信："亲爱的老公，你简直无法相信发生了什么事。几个拿着铲子的人到咱们家把整个后院挖了一遍。"

犯人在回信中写道："亲爱的老婆，现在就是种生菜的最佳时间了。"

钱 这 东 西

It's My Money

A man went into a bank on his hands and knees begging for a loan so he could feed his family.

The banker OK'd the loan and said, "I suggest you go right out and buy some food."

The man said, "Don't tell me what to do with my money!"

是我的钱

一个人到银行跪着恳求一笔贷款来养活家人。

银行职员同意给他贷款，还说："你最好拿了钱就去买点儿吃的。"

那人说："我不需要你来告诉我怎么花我的钱！"

钱 这 东 西

He Knows about the Price

A gorilla walks into a bar. The bartender comes up to him and asks him what he wants.

"A scotch on the rocks, please." He lays a 10 dollar bill on the bar.

The bartender takes the money and goes to fix his drink. He thinks to himself, "Hey, this is a gorilla, he doesn't know about the prices of drinks." and takes 15 cents back. He sets the drink and the money on the bar.

Another bartender asks the first bartender about the gorilla and he says, "Yeah, he's nice. Go talk to him."

他知道价格

一只大猩猩走进酒吧。侍者迎上来问他想要什么。

"请给我来一杯加冰的苏格兰威士忌,"说着他拿出 10 块钱放在吧台上。

侍者拿了钱去调酒。他心想:"他只是一只大猩猩,他对酒的价格没有概念。"于是就拿了 1 毛 5 分的找零,和酒一起放在吧台上。

另一个侍者过来问他大猩猩怎么样,他说:"嗯,挺和善的,去和他聊聊吧。"

钱 这 东 西

The second bartender goes to the gorilla and strikes up a conversation. "Hey there. You know, we don't get too many gorillas in here."

"Well, at $9.85 a drink, I ain't coming back."

那个侍者于是走过去对大猩猩说："嗨，你好啊，你知道吗，我们这可没多少大猩猩来。"

"是吗，9块8毛5一杯酒，我也不会再来了。"

I Want My Dollar Back

A Redneck buys a ticket and wins the lottery.

He goes to claim it. He says, "I want my $20 million."

To which the man verifies his ticket number replied, "No sir. It doesn't work that way. We give you a million today, and then you'll get the rest spread out for the next 19 years.

The Redneck said, "I want all my money RIGHT now! I won it, and I want it."

Again the man patiently explains that he would only get a million that day and the rest during the next 19 years.

把我的钱还给我

一个红脖人买了张彩票还中了奖。

他去兑奖。他说："我要我的 2 000 万。"

负责兑奖的工作人员对他说："不是的，先生。我们不是这样做的。我们的做法是现在先给你 100 万，剩余部分要在接下来的 19 年中分期支付给你。"

红脖人说："我现在就要所有的钱！这是我中奖得的钱，我都要。"

工作人员再次耐心地给他解释当天他只能拿到 100 万，剩下的钱要在以后的 19 年中分期付给。

The Redneck, furious with the man, screams out, "Look, I WANT MY MONEY!! If you're not going to give me all my money right now, THEN I WANT MY DOLLAR BACK!"

红脖人气急败坏地对工作人员叫道："听着，我要我的钱！如果你们不马上给我所有的钱，我就要把我的钱要回来！"

☆ **redneck** /ˈrednek/ *n.* 〈贬〉红脖人（指脖颈晒得红红的美国南部贫苦农民，尤指其中观念狭隘保守者）

☆ **verify** /ˈverɪfaɪ/ *v.* 核实，查对；证明

钱 这 东 西

Lunch-hour

A robber shoved a note under a bank teller's window which said, "I've got you covered. Hand over all the money in the cage and don't say a word."

The teller opened the cash drawer and wrote something down. Then he closed the drawer and returned the note to the robber.

On the back he had written, "Kindly go to the next window; I'm on my lunch-hour."

午休时间

银行劫匪往一个出纳的窗口里塞了一张纸条，上面写着："我正用枪指着你，把里面的钱都递出来，不要说话。"

那个出纳打开现金抽屉后低头写了些什么。然后他关上抽屉，把纸条还给劫匪。

他在纸条背面写了："请去旁边的窗口，我现在在午休。"

☆ shove /ʃʌv/ *v.* 推；乱塞

钱 这 东 西

$chool I$ Great

Dear Dad,

$chool i$ really great. I am making lot$ of friend$ and $tudying very hard. With all my $tuff, I $imply can't think of anything I need, $o if you would like, you can ju$t $end me a card, a$ I would love to hear from you.

Love,

Your $on

Dear Son,

I kNOw that astroNOmy, ecoNOmics, and oceaNOgraphy are eNOugh to keep even an hoNOr student busy. Do NOt forget that the pursuit of kNOwledge is a NOble task, and you can never study eNOugh.

Love,

Dad

学校很棒

亲爱的爸爸：

　　学校真的很棒。我交了很多朋友，学习也很刻苦。我几乎想不出我还缺什么东西，所以如果你愿意，就给我寄一张信用卡吧，我会很高兴收到你的来信。

爱你的

儿子

亲爱的儿子：

　　我知道即使是最优秀的学生学习天文学、经济学和海洋学都会很吃力的。不要忘了追寻知识是无比崇高的，所以学习是无止境的。

爱你的

爸爸

Nothing Is Too Expensive

A man goes to consult a famous specialist about his medical problem.

"How much do I owe you?"

"My fee is fifty dollar," replies the physician.

"Fifty dollar? That's impossible."

"In your case," the doctor replies, "I suppose I could adjust my fee to thirty dollar."

"Thirty dollar for one visit? Ridiculous!"

"Well, then, could you afford twenty dollar?"

"Who has so much money?"

"Look," replies the doctor, growing irritated, "Just give me five dollar and be gone."

怎么都不贵

一个人去找一位著名的专家看病。

"我该付给你多少钱？"

"我的诊费是 50 美元，"医生答道。

"50 块？这太贵了。"

"那么，"医生说，"我想我可以只收你 30 元。"

"一次诊视就要 30 元？这不是漫天要价吗！"

"那么，你付得起 20 元吗？"

"谁有那么多的钱？"

"听着，"医生开始生气了，说，"给我 5 块钱，你就走吧。"

钱 这 东 西

"I can give you two dollar." says the man. "Take it or leave it."

"I don't understand you," says the doctor. "Why did you come to the most expensive doctor?"

"Listen, Doctor," says the patient. "When it comes to my health, nothing is too expensive!"

"我只能给你两块钱，"那人说，"你爱要不要，不要拉倒。"

"我真没法理解你，"医生说，"你为什么要来找最贵的医生看病呢？"

"医生，你听好了，"那人说，"在事关我的健康时，怎么样都不贵的！"

It's Never Been Used

A man who was having heart trouble went to the doctor to see what his options were. Naturally, the doctor recommended a heart transplant.

The man reluctantly agreed, and asked if there were any hearts immediately available, considering that money was no object.

"I do have three hearts," said the doctor. "The first is from an 18-year old kid, non-smoker, athletic, swimmer, with a great diet. He hit his head on the swimming pool and died. It's $100,000. The second is from a marathon

它从来没用过

一个心脏有毛病的人去看医生，医生自然建议他做心脏移植手术。

病人勉强地接受了这个建议，接着又问是否有现成的心脏，价格不是问题。

"我现在确实有三个心脏，"医生说，"第一个是个18岁的小伙子的，他不吸烟，身体健壮，是个游泳运动员，饮食健康。他把头撞在游泳池壁上死了，他的心脏要10万元。第二个是个25岁的马

runner, 25 years old, great condition, very strong. He got hit by a bus. It's $150,000. The third is from a heavy drinker, cigar smoker. It's $500,000."

"Hey, why is that heart so expensive? He lived a terrible life!"

"Yes, but it's from a lawyer. It's never been used!"

拉松运动员的，身体非常棒，死于车祸，他的心脏
要 15 万元。第三个心脏的主人抽烟酗酒，不过他
的心脏要 50 万。"

"喂，为什么他的心脏要这么贵？他的生活糟
透了！"

"这是事实没错，可是他是个律师，他的心根
本就没用过！"

☆ **no object** 不成问题，不在话下

A Smart Businessman

Jack, a smart businessman, talks to his son.

Jack: "I want you to marry a girl of my choice."

Son: "I will choose my own bride."

Jack: "But the girl is Bill Gates's daughter."

Son: "Well, in that case...."

Next Jack approaches Bill Gates.

Jack: "I have a husband for your daughter."

Bill Gates: "But my daughter is too young to marry."

Jack: "But this young man is a vice-president of the World Bank."

Bill Gates: "Ah, in that case...."

精明的商人

杰克是个很精明的商人，他找儿子谈话。

杰克："我想让你娶一个我选的姑娘。"

儿子："我想要自己选新娘。"

杰克："可是这姑娘是比尔·盖茨的女儿。"

儿子："哦，如果是这样的话……"

接着，杰克又去找比尔·盖茨。

杰克："我帮你的女儿选了一个老公。"

比尔·盖茨："可是我女儿还年轻，还不想结婚呢。"

杰克："可是这个年轻人是世界银行的副总裁。"

比尔·盖茨："啊，如果是这样的话……"

Finally Jack goes to see the president of the World Bank.

Jack: "I have a young man to be recommended as a vice-president."

President: "But I already have more vice-presidents than I need."

Jack: "But this young man is Bill Gates's son-in-law."

President: "Ah, in that case...."

This is how business is done!!

钱 这 东 西

最后杰克去见了世界银行的总裁。

杰克："我给你推荐一个年轻人作副总裁。"

总裁："可是我的副总裁已经太多了。"

杰克："可是这个年轻人是比尔·盖茨的女婿。"

总裁："啊，如果是这样的话……"

生意就是这样做成的！！

Lemon Squeeze

The local bar was so sure that its bartender was the strongest man around that they had a standing $1,000 bet. The bartender would squeeze a lemon until all the juice ran into a glass, and hand the lemon to a patron. Anyone who could squeeze one more drop of juice out would win the money. Many people had tried over time but nobody could do it.

One day, a scrawny little man came in, wearing thick glasses and a polyester suit.

"I'd like to try the bet," he said in a tiny, squeaky voice. After the laughter had died down, the bartender grabbed a lemon, and squeezed away. He handed the wrinkled remains of the rind

挤柠檬

当地的酒吧确信他们的侍者是附近地区最强壮的人，于是他们开了一个 1 000 元的赌盘。那个侍者会把一只柠檬的汁水都挤到一个玻璃杯里，然后把这只挤干的柠檬交给顾客，无论谁能再挤出一滴来，就可以赢得那 1 000 元。很多人都来试过了，可是没人能做到。

一天，一个戴着厚厚眼镜、穿着涤纶套装的瘦小男人走了进来。

"我想试一试，"他发出一种尖而细的声音。等大家的笑声减弱了，侍者抓起一只柠檬挤干，然后把剩下的皱巴巴的东西递给那个小个子。当那人攥

钱 这 东 西

to the little man. But the crowd's laughter turned to total silence as the man clenched his fist around the lemon and six drops fell into the glass.

As the crowd cheered, the bartender paid the $1,000 and asked the little man what he did for a living. Was he a lumberjack, or a weightlifter, or what?

"I work for the IRS."

紧拳头又往杯子里挤了六滴柠檬汁时，酒吧里已经变得鸦雀无声。

侍者在大家的欢呼声中付给小个子 1 000 元，又问他是做什么的，是伐木工、举重运动员还是别的什么？

"我在国内收入署工作。"

☆ **squeeze** /skwi:z/ *v.* 榨取；挤

☆ **patron** /'peɪtrən/ *n.* （商店、饭店、旅馆等的）主顾（尤指老主顾）

☆ **scrawny** /'skrɔ:nɪ/ *a.* 骨瘦如柴的；矮小的

☆ **polyester** /ˌpɒlɪ'estə(r)/ *n.* 聚酯纤维，涤纶

☆ **squeaky**/'skwi:kɪ/ *a.* 短促尖声的

☆ **lumberjack** /'lʌmbədʒæk/ *n.* 伐木工

☆ **IRS**（**Internal Revenue Service**）（美国）国内收入署

钱 这 东 西

Six Years

A motorist, driving by a ranch, hit and killed a calf that was crossing the road. The driver went to the owner of the calf and explained what had happened. He then asked what the animal was worth.

"Oh, about $200 today," said the rancher. "But in six years it would have been worth $900. So $900 is what I'm out."

The motorist sat down and wrote out a check and handed it to the rancher.

"Here," he said, "is the check for $900. It's postdated six years from now."

6 年

一个人开车路过一个农场，撞死了一头正在过马路的牛。他去找牛的主人说明情况，然后他问这牛价值多少。

"它现在值 200 元，"农场主说，"但是 6 年后，它就值 900 元了，所以我损失了 900 元。"

开车人坐下来签了一张支票，递给农场主。

"给你，"他说，"这是 900 元的支票，兑付的日期是 6 年后。"

☆ **postdate** /ˌpəʊstˈdeɪt/ v. 在（支票、信件、文件等）上填写比实际晚的日期

钱 这 东 西

Show You the True Money

A fool and his money are asked to go everywhere.

A fool and his money are soon elected.

A fool and his money are soon popular.

A fool and his money is my kind of customer.

If money's the root of all evil, why do churches want it?

All I ask is to prove that money can't make me happy.

Come to Florida, bring money, BUT GET THE HECK OFF OUR BEACH!

告诉你钱的真相

一个有钱的傻瓜被邀请去世界各地。

一个有钱的傻瓜很快就被选上了。

一个有钱的傻瓜很快就家喻户晓。

一个有钱的傻瓜是我的顾客。

如果钱是万恶之源，那么教堂要它来做什么？

我所问的就是要证明钱不能使我幸福。

带着钱到佛罗里达来，但是离我们的海滩
远些！

钱 这 东 西

Even the blind can see money.

Life is a game. Money is how we keep score.

Money burns a hole in my pocket ... how about yours?

Money is like an arm or leg, use it or lose it.

Money is the root of all bills.

Money may buy "friendship," but it cannot buy love.

Expert — Someone who knows less, but makes more money.

Money Talks — and it usually says NO!!

Never forget a friend, especially if he owes you money.

钱 这 东 西

就是瞎子也能看见钱。

人生是一场比赛，钱就是我们得了多少分数。

钱把我的口袋烧了个洞，你的呢？

钱就像是你的胳膊腿，用掉或是失去。

钱是所有的账单之源。

钱也许能买到"友谊"，但是买不到爱。

专家——那些懂得更少却赚更多的钱的人。

钱会说话，只是通常说的是"不"！！

永远不要忘记朋友，尤其是那些欠你钱的。

钱 这 东 西

Political Motto: I had some morals; sold them for money.

This country has the best politicians money can buy.

Time and Money — Two things we don't have enough of.

You infernal machine! Give me a soda or my money back!

Alimony? ... sounds kind like all yer money.

No one kills over drugs ... They kill over money.

钱 这 东 西

政治箴言:我有道德,给钱就卖。

这个国家里有花钱能买到的最好的政治家。

时间和金钱——我们永远缺少的两样东西。

你这该死的机器!给我一瓶苏打水,不然就把我的钱吐出来!

扶养费? 听起来就像是在说"你全部的钱"。

没有人死于吸毒……他们都是让钱弄死的。

☆ **burn a hole in one's pocket** (钱等)在口袋里留不住,大手大脚

☆ **money talks** 金钱万能

☆ **motto** /ˈmɒtəʊ/ n. 座右铭,箴言,格言

☆ **infernal** /ɪnˈfɜːnəl/ a. 地狱(般)的;可恨的

☆ **alimony** /ˈælɪmənɪ/ n.【律】(经法院判决在分居或离婚以前或以后男方付给妻子或前妻的)扶养费

Fifty Dollars Is Fifty Dollars

Ferber and his wife Martha went to the fair every year. Every year Ferber would say, "Martha, I'd like to ride in that there airplane."

And every year Martha would say, "I know Ferber, but that airplane ride costs fifty dollars, and fifty dollars is fifty dollars."

One year Ferber and Martha went to the fair and Ferber said, "Martha, I'm 71 years old. If I don't ride that airplane this year I may never get another chance."

Martha replied, "Ferber, that airplane ride costs fifty dollars, and fifty dollars is fifty dollars."

50 块钱就是 50 块钱

费伯和妻子玛莎每年都去市集。每年费伯都会说："玛莎，我想坐那架飞机。"

而玛莎每年都会这样回答他："费伯，我知道你想坐那架飞机，可是坐飞机要花 50 块钱呢，50 块钱啊。"

一年，费伯和玛莎又来到市集，费伯说："玛莎，我已经 71 岁了，我今年要是再不坐飞机的话，我就没机会坐了。"

玛莎答道："费伯，坐那架飞机要花 50 块钱呢，50 块钱啊。"

The pilot overheard them and said, "Folks, I'll make you a deal, I'll take you both up for a ride. If you can stay quiet for the entire ride and not say one word, I won't charge you, but if you say one word it's fifty dollars."

Ferber and Martha agreed and up they went. The pilot did all kinds of twists and turns, rolls and dives, but not a word was heard. He did all his tricks over again, but still not a word.

They landed and the pilot turned to Ferber, "By golly, I did everything I could think of to get you to yell out, but you didn't."

Ferber replied, "Well, I was gonna say something when Martha fell out, but ten dollars is ten dollars."

飞行员听到了他们的谈话，走上前来说："两位，我跟你们做个交易吧，我让你们两个都坐飞机。如果你们在整个飞行期间都能不说一句话，我就不收你们的钱。可是如果你们说了一个字，我就要收 50 块钱了。"

费伯和玛莎同意了，他们上了飞机。飞行员做了各种翻滚和俯冲的动作，可是他没听到他们发出一声。于是他把所有的特技动作又来了一遍，可还是没听他们吭一声。

着陆后，飞行员对费伯说："天哪，我做了所有的特技，我想你们会叫出来的，可是你们竟然一声没吭。"

费伯答道："玛莎掉出去时，我是想说一声的，可是要 50 块钱呢，50 块钱啊。"

Less Knowledge More Money

Dilbert's Theorem on Salary states that Engineers, Teachers, Programmers and Scientists can never earn as much salary as business executives and sales people. This theorem can now be supported by a mathematical equation based on the following three postulates:

Postulate 1: Knowledge is Power (Knowledge = Power)

Postulate 2: Time is Money (Time = Money)

Postulate 3: (as every Physics student knows) Power = Work / Time

知识越少，钱越多

迪尔伯特薪水定律说工程师、教师、程序员和科学家永远不可能比商人和销售人员挣得多。现在这条定律能用建立在下面三条假设基础上的数学等式证明了。

假设一：知识就是力量（知识＝力量〈功率〉）

假设二：时间就是金钱（时间＝金钱）

假设三：（每个学过物理的学生都知道这个物理公式）功率＝功／时间

钱 这 东 西

It therefore follows:

Knowledge = Work / Time

and since Time = Money,

we have: Knowledge = Work / Money

Solving for Money, we get:

Money = Work / Knowledge

Thus, as Knowledge approaches zero, Money approaches infinity, regardless of the amount of Work done.

这样我们就能得出下面这个等式：

知识＝功〈工作〉/时间

因为"时间＝金钱"

我们可以得出：知识＝功/金钱

把"金钱"移到等式左侧，我们得出：

金钱＝功〈工作〉/知识

因此，无论你做多少工作，当你的"知识"越少时，你的"金钱"就越接近于无限大。

☆ **theorem** /ˈθɪərəm/ *n.* 定理；原理；理论

☆ **postulate** /ˈpɒstjʊleɪt/ *n.* 假定，假设

钱 这 东 西

What Kind of Salesman
Are You?

A real estate salesman had just closed his first deal, only to discover that the piece of land he had sold was completely under water.

"That customer's going to come back here pretty mad," he said to his boss. "Should I give him his money back?"

"Money back?" roared the boss. "What kind of salesman are you? Get out there and sell him a houseboat!"

你算什么销售员？

一个地产销售员刚做成他的第一笔生意，却发现自己刚卖掉的那块地完全淹在水下。

"那个买主会回来找我的，他会气疯的，"他对老板说，"我是不是该把钱还给他？"

"把钱还给他？"老板咆哮着说，"你算什么推销员？去卖给他一座水上住宅！"

钱 这 东 西

God Will Pay the Bill

A man was brought to the hospital, and taken quickly in for emergency surgery. The operation went well, and as the groggy man regained consciousness, he was reassured by a Sister of Mercy, who was waiting by his bed.

"Mr. Smith, you're going to be just fine," said the nun, gently patting his hand. "We do need to know, however, how you intend to pay for your stay here. Are you covered by insurance?"

"No, I'm not," the man whispered hoarsely.

"Can you pay in cash?" persisted the nun.

上帝会付账

一个人进了医院后立刻就被送去做急诊手术。手术一切正常，当他从昏昏沉沉中醒来时，一个修女正在床边照顾他。

"史密斯先生，你会好起来的，"修女轻轻地拍着他的手说，"但是，我们现在要知道，你准备怎么支付这里的医疗费用。你上保险了吗？"

"不，我没上保险，"他用嘶哑的嗓音低声说道。

"那么你能用现金支付吗？"修女接着问。

钱 这 东 西

"I'm afraid I cannot, Sister."

"Well, do you have any close relatives?" the nun essayed.

"Just my sister in New York," he volunteered. "But she's a spinster nun."

"Oh, I must correct you, Mr. Smith. Nuns are not 'spinsters'; they are married to God."

"Really ... wonderful," said Smith. "In that case, you can send the bill to my brother-in-law!"

"我恐怕不能，修女。"

"那么，你有近亲吗?"修女继续问道。

"只有一个妹妹在纽约，"他说，"可她是个'老处女'修女。"

"噢，史密斯先生，我一定得更正你，修女不是'老处女'，她们是嫁给了上帝。"

"是吗……这太棒了，"史密斯说，"如果是那样的话，你们可以把账单寄给我妹夫!"

☆ **groggy** /ˈgrɒgɪ/ *a.* 摇摇晃晃的；昏昏沉沉的

☆ **reassure** /ˌriːəˈʃʊə(r)/ *v.* 向…再保证；安慰

☆ **Sister of Mercy** （从事慈善教育事业的天主教女修会）慈光会的修女

☆ **hoarsely** /ˈhɔːslɪ/ *ad.* 嗓音嘶哑地

☆ **essay** /ˈeseɪ/ *v.* 作…尝试；企图

☆ **spinster** /ˈspɪnstə(r)/ *n.* 老处女；未婚妇女

Forgotten Pillowcases

A stingy old lawyer who had been diagnosed with a terminal illness was determined to prove wrong the saying, "You can't take it with you."

After much thought and consideration, the old ambulance chaser finally figured out how to take at least some of his money with him when he died.

He instructed his wife to go to the bank and withdraw enough money to fill two pillowcases. He then directed her to take the bags of money to the attic and leave them directly above his bed.

忘了拿的枕套

一个吝啬的老律师被诊断出得了不治之症。于是他决定要证明"生不带来，死不带去"这句老话说错了。

经过深思熟虑，这个怂恿事故受伤者起诉的律师终于想出了让自己在死的时候至少能带走一部分钱的方法。

他要妻子去银行取出能塞满两只枕套的现金。然后又让她把装满钱的枕套放在阁楼上正对着他的床的位置上。

His plan: When he passed away, he would reach out and grab the bags on his way to heaven.

Several weeks after the funeral, the deceased lawyer's wife, up in the attic cleaning, came upon the two forgotten pillowcases stuffed with cash.

"Oh, that darned old fool," she exclaimed. "I knew he should have had me put the money in the basement."

他的如意算盘是：他死了的时候，就能在去往天堂的路上抓起那两只钱袋。

葬礼过后几个星期，律师的妻子在打扫阁楼的时候发现了那两只装满了钱的枕套。

"噢，这个下地狱的老笨蛋，"她大叫道，"我就知道他本该让我把钱放在地下室里的。"

☆ **stingy** /ˈstɪndʒɪ/ a. 吝啬的，小气的

☆ **terminal** /ˈtɜːmɪnəl/ a. 末期的；致命的

☆ **ambulance chaser** 〈美口〉怂恿事故受伤者起诉的律师

钱 这 东 西

What Money Can Buy

MONEY

It can buy a House

But not a Home

It can buy a Bed

But not Sleep

It can buy a Clock

But not Time

It can buy you a Book

But not Knowledge

钱能买什么

钱

能买到房子

却买不来家

能买到床

却买不来睡眠

能买到钟

却买不来时间

能买到书

却买不来知识

钱 这 东 西

It can buy you a Position

But not Respect

It can buy you Medicine

But not Health

It can buy you Blood

But not Life

It can buy you Sex

But not Love

Money isn't everything

It often causes pain and suffering

钱这东西

能买到地位

却买不来尊敬

能买到药

却买不来健康

能买到血

却买不来生命

能买到性

却买不来爱

钱不是一切

钱常会给人带来悲伤和痛苦

钱 这 东 西

I tell you this

cause I'm your friend

and want to take away

your pain and suffering

So send me all your money

and I will suffer for you

I ACCEPT CASH, MONEY ORDERS, PER-
SONAL CHECKS, CASHIERS CHECKS, BAGS
OF GOLD, BARS OF PLATINUM, ETC....

我告诉你这些

是因为你是我朋友

并且想帮你祛除

你的悲伤和痛苦

所以把你所有的钱都给我吧

这样我就能代你忍受这些悲伤和痛苦了

我接受现金、汇票、个人支票、（银行）本票、
黄金、铂金，等等等等……

Honesty

An investment counselor decided to go out on her own. She was shrewd and diligent, so business kept coming in, and pretty soon she realized that she needed an in-house counsel. She began to interview young lawyers.

"As I'm sure you can understand," she started off with one of the first applicants, "in a business like this, our personal integrity must be beyond question."

She leaned forward. "Mr. Peterson, are you an 'honest' lawyer?"

"Honest?" replied the job prospect. "Let me tell you something about honest. Why, I'm

诚　实

　　一个投资顾问决定自己干，她够精明和勤奋，所以她的生意蒸蒸日上。不久以后她就意识到自己需要一个法律顾问。于是她开始面试年轻的律师。

　　"我确信你一定能够理解，"她开始和第一个应聘者面谈，"做我们这一行的，他个人的诚实信用一定要毫无瑕疵。"

　　她向前欠了欠身，"那么，彼得森先生，你是个'诚实的'律师吗?"

　　"诚实吗?"应聘者答道，"让我来告诉你一件有关于诚实的事。是的，我很诚实，我父亲借给我

so honest that my father lent me $15,000 for my education, and I paid back every penny the minute I tried my very first case."

"Impressive. And what sort of case was that?"

The young lawyer squirmed in his seat and admitted, "He sued me for the money."

15 000 元钱让我上学，而我在办理我的第一个案子的时候就把所有的钱都还清了。"

"真是令人钦佩。顺便问一下，那是个什么案子？"

年轻的律师局促不安地在椅子上扭动着，说："他起诉我要我还钱。"

☆ **in-house** /ˈɪnˈhaʊs/ *a.* 存在于机构内部的；有关机构内部事务的

☆ **integrity** /ɪnˈtegrətɪ/ *n.* 正直；诚实

☆ **squirm** /skwɜːm/ *v.* 扭动；局促不安

Paying the Dentist in Advance

As soon as the dentist asked the patient to sit down, he pulled out his wallet.

Seeing this the dentist said, "Please don't, you don't need to pay me now."

The patient answered: "Pay you? No! I just want to count my money before I'm unconscious!"

提前付钱给牙医

牙医要病人坐下时，病人掏出了自己的钱包。

牙医看见了，说："不用，你不用现在就付钱给我。"

病人答道："付钱给你？才不是呢！我只是想在失去知觉前数数我到底有多少钱！"

Fifty Cents

A man walks into a bar and yells, "Bartender, give me twenty shots of your best brandy!"

The bartender pours the shots and the man drinks them down one at a time, as fast as he can.

The bartender says, "Wow, I never saw anyone drink that fast."

The man replies by saying, "Well, you'd drink fast if you had what I have."

The bartender says, "Oh my god, what do you have??!!"

The man says, "Fifty cents."

5 毛钱

一个人走进酒吧叫道:"侍者,给我来 20 杯你们这儿最好的白兰地!"

侍者给他倒好酒,只见那人一口一杯,飞快地喝完了。

侍者说:"哇,我从没见过喝酒喝得像你这么快的。"

那人答道:"是吗,你要是有我有的这点儿东西,你也会喝这么快的。"

侍者说:"天哪,你有什么??!!"

那人说:"5 毛钱。"

钱这东西

How to Save Money

Three engineers and three accountants are traveling by train to a conference.

At the station, the three accountants each buy tickets and watch as the three engineers buy only a single ticket.

"How are three people going to travel on only one ticket?" asks an accountant.

"Watch and you'll see," answers an engineer.

They all board the train. The accountants take their respective seats but all three engineers cram into a restroom and close the door behind them.

怎样省钱

三个工程师和三个会计一起坐火车去参加一个会议。

到了火车站，三个会计每人买了一张火车票，可他们注意到三个工程师只买了一张票。

"你们三个人怎么能只用一张票乘车呢？"一个会计问道。

"你们看着吧，"一个工程师答道。

他们都上了火车，会计们坐到了他们各自的座位上，工程师们却全挤进了一个洗手间并关上了门。

Shortly after the train has departed, the conductor comes around collecting tickets. He knocks on the restroom door and says, "Ticket, please."

The door opens just a crack and a single arm emerges with a ticket in hand. The conductor takes it and moves on.

The accountants saw this and agreed it was quite a clever idea. So after the conference, the accountants decide to copy the engineers on the return trip and save some money.

When they get to the station, they buy a single ticket for the return trip. To their astonishment, the engineers don't buy a ticket at all.

不一会儿，列车启动了，列车员走过来查票。他敲了敲洗手间的门，说："请出示车票。"

门打开了一条缝，一只手拿着车票伸了出来。列车员检了票，就走开了。

会计们看后觉得这真是个好办法。于是会后他们决定在回程的火车上照样做，好省下些钱。

到火车站后，三个会计买了一张票。可让他们吃惊的是，这回工程师们根本连一张票也没买。

"How are you going to travel without a ticket?" says one perplexed accountant.

"Watch and you'll see," answers an engineer.

When they board the train the three accountants cram into a restroom and the three engineers cram into another one nearby.

The train departs.

Shortly afterward, one of the engineers leaves his restroom and walks over to the restroom where the accountants are hiding. He knocks on the door and says, "Ticket, please."

"你们三个人怎么能不用车票就乘车呢?"一个困惑不解的会计问道。

"你们看着吧,"一个工程师答道。

他们都上了火车,三个会计挤进了一个洗手间,三个工程师挤进了另一个。

火车开动了。

不一会儿,一个工程师走出来,走到会计们藏身的那个洗手间门口,敲了敲门,说:"请出示车票。"

钱 这 东 西

We Can't Wait That Long

A customer sent an order to a distributor for a large amount of goods totaling a great deal of money.

The distributor noticed that the previous bill hadn't been paid. The collections manager left a voice mail for them saying, "We can't ship your new order until you pay for the last one."

The next day the collections manager received a collect phone call, "Please cancel the order. We can't wait that long."

我们等不了那么久

一个主顾发了一份订单给分销商要一大批货，这些货物值许多钱。

分销商注意到这个主顾的前一笔账单还没付。于是经理发了一个声音邮件给这个主顾，说："我方要等你方付清上一笔未结款项后才能发货。"

第二天，经理接到了一个受方付费的电话，打来电话的人说："请取消订单，我们等不了那么久。"

Grass Eater

A man was riding in the back of his limousine when he saw a man eating grass by the roadside. He ordered his driver to stop and he got out to investigate.

"Why are you eating grass?" he asked the man.

"I don't have any money for food," the poor man replied.

"Oh, please come to my house!"

"But sir, I have a wife and four children...."

"Bring them along!" the rich man said.

吃草的人

一个人坐在他的高级轿车里看到一个人正在路边吃草。他要司机停了车，然后下车去查看。

"你为什么吃草？"他问道。

"因为我没钱买食物。"那穷苦的人答道。

"噢，那到我家来吧!"

"可是，先生，我还有妻子和四个孩子……"

"把他们都带来!"那富人说。

They all climbed into the limo. Once underway, the poor fellow said, "Sir, you are too kind. Thank you for taking all of us in."

The rich man replied, "No, you don't understand. The grass at my house is over three feet tall!"

钱 这 东 西

他们都坐进了轿车里。走在路上时，穷人说："先生，你真是太好了，感谢你把我们全家都带上了。"

富人答道："不是的，你不明白，我家里的草都长得足有 3 英尺高了！"

Gold in Heaven

There once was a rich man who was near death. He was very grieved because he had worked so hard for his money and wanted to be able to take it with him to heaven. So he began to pray that he might be able to take some of his wealth with him.

An angel heard his plea and appeared to him. "Sorry, but you can't take your wealth with you."

The man begged the angel to speak to God to see if He might bend the rules. The man continued to pray that his wealth could follow him.

The angel reappeared and informed the man that God had decided to allow him to take one suitcase with him. Overjoyed, the man gathered

金子在天堂

从前有个有钱人快要死了。他很伤心，因为他一生都在努力赚钱，就想能把这些钱都带到天堂去。于是他开始祈祷能带着自己的财富走。

一个天使听到了他的祈祷，出现在他的面前："我很抱歉，你不能带着你的钱。"

那人求天使帮忙，于是天使去找上帝，看他能否修改规定。那人继续祈祷自己能带着钱走。

天使又来了，告诉他上帝允许他随身带一只箱子。那人万分高兴，找到一只最大号的箱子，装满了金条，放在床边。

his largest suitcase and filled it with pure gold bars and placed it beside his bed.

Soon afterward, he died and showed up at the gates of heaven to greet St. Peter.

St. Peter, seeing the suitcase, said, "Hold on, you can't bring that in here!"

The man explained to St. Peter that he had permission and asked him to verify his story with the Lord.

Sure enough, St. Peter checked it out, came back and said, "You're right. You are allowed one carry-on bag, but I'm supposed to check its contents before letting it through."

St. Peter opened the suitcase to inspect the worldly items that the man found too precious to leave behind and exclaimed, "You brought pavement?"

钱 这 东 西

不久以后，那人死了，来到了天堂门前，见到了圣彼得。

圣彼得看到他的箱子，说："等一下，你不能把这东西带进来！"

那人告诉圣彼得自己是得到允许的，并请他去找上帝证实。

圣彼得得到了肯定的答复，出来对他说："不错，你是可以带一件随身的行李，不过，让你进去之前，我要先检查一下你箱子里的东西。"

圣彼得打开箱子检视里面装着的世俗人觉得珍贵得无法抛开的东西后，叫道："你带了地砖来？"

錢 這 東 西

I Already Paid

A man in a bar had a couple of beers, and the bartender told him he owed 4 dollars.

"But I paid, don't you remember?" said the customer.

"Okay," said the bartender. "If you say you paid, you did."

The man then went outside and told a friend that the bartender couldn't keep track of his customers' bills. The second man then rushed in and ordered a beer. When it came time to pay he pulled the same stunt.

The barkeep replied, "If you say you paid, I'll take your word for it."

Soon the customer went into the street, saw an old friend, and told him how to get free drinks.

我付过账了

一个人在酒吧喝了几杯啤酒，侍者对他说他的酒钱是 4 元。

"可是我已经付过了，你不记得了吗?"那人说。

"好吧，"侍者说，"既然你说你付过了，就算付过了吧。"

那人跑出去告诉了一个朋友说那个酒吧的侍者记不清顾客付账的情况。于是他的朋友也跑去要了一杯啤酒，到该付账的时候，他也要了同样的花招。

侍者说:"既然你说你付过了，我就相信你。"

不久后，这人走在街上遇到了一个老朋友，就又告诉他这种免费喝酒的方法。

The man hurried into the bar and began to drink highballs when, suddenly, the bartender leaned over and said, "You know, a funny thing happened in here tonight. Two men were drinking beer, neither paid and both claimed that they did. The next guy who tries that is going to get punched right in the nose."

"Don't bother me with your troubles," the final patron responded. "Just give me my change and I'll be on my way."

这位老朋友也赶快跑到酒吧里喝高杯酒。突然，侍者欠身过来说："你知道吗，今天晚上这里有个好笑的事，前面有两个人喝了酒不付钱还声称自己付过了，再有人这样做的话，我会照着他的鼻子给一拳的。"

"别拿你的麻烦事来烦我，"这第三位答道，"赶快找我钱，我要走了。"

☆ stunt /stʌnt/ *n.* 绝技；花招；噱头

☆ **pull a stunt** 要花招

☆ **highball** /ˈhaɪbɔːl/ *n.* 高杯酒（用威士忌或白兰地等烈酒掺水或汽水加冰块制成的饮料，盛在高玻璃杯内饮用）

I Don't Know Either

A scientist gets on a train to go to New York. His cabin also has a farmer in it. To pass the time the scientist decides to play a game with the guy.

"I will ask you a question and if you get it wrong, you have to pay me 1 dollar. Then you ask me a question, and if I get it wrong, you get 10 dollars. You ask me a question first."

The farmer thinks for a while. "I know. What has three legs, takes 10 hours to climb up a palm tree, and 10 seconds to get back down?"

The scientist is confused and thinks long and hard about the question. Finally, the train ride is coming to an end.

我也不知道

一个科学家坐火车去纽约，他的这节车厢里还有一个农民。为了打发时间，科学家决定和农民做个游戏。

"我问你一个问题，如果你答错了，你给我 1 块钱。然后你问我一个问题，如果我答错了，我给你 10 块钱。现在你先问我一个问题吧。"

农民想了一会儿，"有了，什么东西长着三条腿，要花 10 个小时爬上一棵棕榈树，下来却只要 10 秒钟？"

科学家被搞糊涂了，他努力地想啊想啊。最后，火车到终点了。

As it pulls into the station, the scientist takes out 10 dollars and gives it to the farmer. "I don't know. What has 3 legs, takes 10 hours to get up a palm tree and 10 seconds to get back down?"

The farmer takes the 10 dollars and puts it into his pocket. He then takes out 1 dollar and hands it to the scientist.

"I don't know."

火车进站的时候,科学家拿出 10 块钱给农民。"我不知道了。这个长着三条腿,花 10 个小时爬上一棵棕榈树,下来却只要 10 秒钟的到底是什么东西?"

农民接过 10 块钱放进口袋,又掏出 1 块钱递给科学家。

"我不知道。"

钱 这 东 西

Same Old Stuff

A one dollar bill met a 20 dollar bill and said, "Hey, where've you been? I haven't seen you around here much."

The twenty answered, "I've been hanging out at the casinos, went on a cruise and did the rounds of the ship, back to the United States for awhile, went to a couple of baseball games, to the mall, that kind of stuff. How about you?"

The one dollar bill said, "You know, same old stuff, church, church, church."

老 样 子

一张 1 美元的钞票遇见了一张 20 美元的钞票，它说："你好啊，你去哪儿了？最近没怎么见到你。"

20 美元钞票答："我常在赌场里晃来晃去的，还上了一艘船巡游了一圈，刚回到美国，去了几场棒球赛，又去商场，就这些地方呗。你怎么样？"

1 美元的钞票说："你知道的，还是老样子，教堂、教堂，还是教堂。"

Hit Him Again

A crumbling old church building needed remodeling, so, during his sermon, the preacher made an impassioned appeal looking directly at the richest man in town.

At the end of the sermon, the rich man stood up and announced, "Pastor, I will contribute $1,000."

Just then, plaster fell from the ceiling and struck the rich man on the shoulder.

He promptly stood back up and shouted, "Pastor, I will increase my donation to $5,000."

Before he could sit back down, plaster fell on him again, this time he virtually screamed, "Pastor, I will double my last pledge."

再砸他呀

一座摇摇欲坠的老教堂需要重建了。所以，在布道中，牧师对着城里最富有的人慷慨激昂地呼吁了一番。

布道结束时，那个富有的人站起来宣布说："牧师，我捐献 1 000 元。"

就在这时，从房顶上掉下来一块灰泥正好砸在他的肩膀上。

他立刻又站起来叫道："牧师，我要多捐些，我捐 5 000 元。"

还没等他坐下，灰泥又落在他的身上，这次他已经是惊声尖叫了："牧师，我捐 10 000 元。"

钱 这 东 西

He sat down, and a larger chunk of plaster fell on his head.

He stood up once more and hollered, "Pastor, I will give $20,000!"

This prompted a deacon to shout, "Hit him again, Lord! Hit him again!"

他坐下，又一大块灰泥掉在他的头上。

他再一次站起来，大喊道："牧师，我捐 20 000 元！"

这一切使得一个执事叫了出来："再来啊，主！再砸他呀！"

☆ **crumble** /'krʌmbl/ v. 崩溃，瓦解

☆ **remodel** /ˌriːˈmɒdəl/ v. 改建；重新做

☆ **impassioned** /ɪmˈpæʃənd/ a. 充满激情的；激昂的

☆ **chunk** /tʃʌŋk/ n. 厚片，大块

☆ **holler** /ˈhɒlə(r)/ v.（为唤起注意或在痛苦等时）叫喊，嚷嚷

☆ **deacon** /ˈdiːkən/ n.【宗】（基督教新教的）执事

Send Him the Account

A doctor and a lawyer were attending a cocktail party when the doctor was approached by a man who asked advice on how to handle his stomach ulcer. The doctor mumbled some medical advice, then turned to the lawyer and asked, "How do you handle the situation when you are asked for advice during a social function?"

"Just send an account for such advice," replied the lawyer.

On the next morning the doctor arrived at his surgery and issued the stomach-ulcer-stricken man a $60 account.

That afternoon he received a $100 account from the lawyer.

把账单寄给他

一位医生和一名律师在参加一个鸡尾酒会。这时，一个人走上前来问医生怎样缓解他的胃溃疡。医生含混不清地说了几句，然后转向律师问道："像这种在公共场合向你咨询的情况，你是怎么处理的？"

"我会把咨询费的账单寄给他，"律师答。

第二天早上，医生一到诊所就签了一张 60 元的账单寄给那个胃溃疡的人。

当天下午，他收到了律师寄来的 100 元咨询费的账单。

☆ **ulcer** /ˈʌlsə(r)/ *n.* 【医】溃疡

☆ **mumble** /ˈmʌmbl/ *v.* 含糊地说，咕哝

钱 这 东 西

You'll Soon Get Used to It

An man died and left his son a lot of money. But the son was a foolish young man, and he quickly spent all the money, so that soon he had nothing left.

Of course, when that happened, all his friends left him. When he was quite poor and alone, he went to see a kind, clever old man and often helped people when they had troubles.

"My money has finished and my friends have gone," said the young man. "What will happen to me now?"

"Don't worry, young man," answered the old man. "Everything will soon be all right again. Wait, and you will soon feel much happier."

你不久就会习惯的

一个人死了，留给他儿子一大笔钱。可是他儿子是个愚蠢的年轻人，他很快就花光了所有的钱，不久后就一文不名了。

当然，在这种时候，他所有的朋友都离开了他。在他又穷又孤独的时候，他去见了一位常帮人脱困的慈祥又智慧的老者。

"我没钱了，我的朋友们也都跑了，"年轻人说，"我还能怎么样？"

"别担心，年轻人，"老者答道，"一切都会好起来的，等着瞧吧，不久后你就会再快乐起来的。"

The young man was very glad. "Am I going to get rich again then?" he asked the old man.

"No, I didn't mean that," said the old man. "I meant that you would soon get used to being poor and to having no friends."

钱 这 东 西

年轻人听了很高兴。"那么，我又会有钱了吗？"他问老者。

"不是的，我不是那个意思，"老者说，"我的意思是你不久后就会习惯于没钱和没朋友的日子了。"

Nickel or Dime?

Little Johnny used to hang out at the local corner store. The owner didn't know what Johnny's problem was, but the older boys would constantly tease him.

They would play a game with him, sometimes they would offer Johnny his choice between a nickel (5 cents) and a dime (10 cents) in their open palms and Johnny would always take the nickel — they said, because it was bigger.

One day after Johnny grabbed the nickel, the store owner took him aside and said, "Johnny, those boys are making fun of you.

5 分钱还是 10 分钱？

　　小约翰尼过去常在街角的商店附近闲逛。店主不知道小约翰尼有什么问题，但是年龄大些的男孩子们经常嘲弄他。

　　他们和他玩一种游戏作弄他，有时他们在掌心上放一个 5 分镍币和一个 10 分硬币让约翰尼选。约翰尼总是选 5 分的。他们说是因为 5 分镍币个儿大。

　　一天，在约翰尼又拿了5分镍币后，店主把他叫到一边问："约翰尼，那些孩子在作弄你。你不

Don't you know that a dime is twice as good as a nickel? Are you grabbing the nickel because it's bigger, or what?"

Slowly, Johnny turned toward the storeowner and a big grin appeared on his face and Johnny said, "Well, if I took the dime, they'd stop doing it, and so far I have saved $20!"

知道十分硬币要值两个 5 分镍币吗？你选 5 分镍币
是因为它大吗？"

约翰尼慢吞吞转向店主，咧嘴笑着说："是这
样的，如果我拿了 10 分硬币，他们就不会再跟我
玩了。事实上，到现在我已经赚了 20 块钱了！"

☆ **tease** /ti:z/ *v.* 戏弄；取笑

☆ **nickel** /ˈnɪkəl/ *n.*（美国和加拿大的）5 分镍币

☆ **dime** /daɪm/ *n.*（美国和加拿大的）10 分铸币

☆ **make fun of somebody** 拿某人开玩笑，取笑某人

钱 这 东 西

How You Made Money

A young man asked an old rich man how he made his money.

The old guy fingered his worsted wool vest and said, "Well, son, it was 1930. The depth of the Great Depression. I was down to my last nickel."

"I invested that nickel in an apple. I spent the entire day polishing the apple and, at the end of the day, I sold the apple for ten cents."

"The next morning, I invested those ten cents in two apples. I spent the entire day polishing them and sold them at 6:00 p.m. for 20 cents. I continued this system for a month, by the end of which I'd accumulated a fortune of $1.58."

你怎么赚的钱

一个年轻人问一位富有的老人是怎样赚到钱的。

老人轻抚着自己的精纺毛背心，说道："孩子，是这样的。那是 1930 年，大萧条时期，我就只剩下 5 分钱。"

"我用这 5 分钱买了一个苹果，然后用一整天的时间把这只苹果擦得光洁漂亮，到晚上，我把它卖了一毛钱。"

"第二天早上，我用这一毛钱买了两个苹果并用一整天把它们擦得光洁漂亮，下午 6 点钟时我把它们卖了两毛钱。如此以往，一个月后，我积攒了一块五毛八。"

钱 这 东 西

"And that's how you built an empire?" the boy asked.

"Heavens, no!" the man replied. "Then my wife's father died and left us five million dollars."

"你就是这样发家致富的?"年轻人问。

"当然不是!"老人答道,"后来,我的老丈人死了,留给我们 500 万。"

钱这东西

Too Much Money

On their sixtieth wedding anniversary, the wealthy old man said to his wife, "Honey, for our sixtieth, I'm going to buy you a 60-karat diamond. I'll hold a party for sixty friends, and we'll celebrate in a five-star restaurant."

She looked at him. "I don't want those things," she said. "All I want is a divorce."

"Oh, no!" he said. "That much money I'm not ready to spend!"

钱 太 多

结婚 60 周年纪念日那天，富有的丈夫对妻子说："亲爱的，为了纪念我们结婚 60 周年，我要给你买一枚 60 克拉的钻戒。我们还要在一家五星级饭店举行晚会，宴请 60 位朋友共同为我们庆贺。"

她看着他，"我不想要这些东西，"她说，"我就要和你离婚。"

"噢，不要！"他说，"我还没准备花那么多钱呢！"

钱 这 东 西

Ten Dollar

The teacher asked Tom, "Why did you come to school so late this morning?"

"Someone lost ten dollar," answered Tom.

"Oh, now I know, you helped him find the money," the teacher said.

"No, I stood on the money until the person went away," was Tom's reply.

10 美元

老师问汤姆："你今天早上为什么迟到了？"

"有人丢了 10 块钱，"汤姆答。

"哦，我知道了，你一定是帮他找到了他丢的钱，"老师说。

"不是的，我一直站在那钱上等他走开，"汤姆答。

钱 这 东 西

Congratulations

My Dearest Susan,

Sweetie of my heart. I've been so desolate ever since I broke off our engagement. Simply devastated. Won't you please consider coming back to me? You hold a place in my heart no other woman can fill. I can never marry another woman quite like you. I need you so much. Won't you forgive me and let us make a new beginning? I love you so.

Yours always and truly,

John

P. S. Congratulations on you winning the state lottery.

恭 喜

最亲爱的苏珊：

　　我的宝贝。我推掉我们的婚约后孑然一身，完全的身心交瘁。你能否考虑回到我的身边？你在我心中的地位没有其他女人可以替代。我再也不会找到一个像你这样的女人了。我太需要你了。你能不能原谅我，让我们重新开始？我爱你。

　　　　　　　　　　　你永远真挚的

　　　　　　　　　　　约翰

　　又及：恭喜你中了全国彩票的大奖。

☆ **desolate** /ˈdesələt/ *a.* 被遗弃的；孤独凄凉的

☆ **break off** 绝交，断绝友好关系

☆ **engagement** /ɪnˈɡeɪdʒmənt/ *n.* 订婚，婚约

☆ **devastate** /ˈdevəsteɪt/ *n.* 压倒，使垮掉

☆ **P. S.** （postscript） （信末签名后的）附笔，又及

☆ **lottery** /ˈlɒtərɪ/ *n.* 抽彩给奖法

I Have Money

I was in Las Vegas, when a man walked up to me and said, "Sir, do you have a extra $20, my wife needs an operation that costs $1,000. I have $980 and just need the last $20."

I thought about and I asked the man, "How will I know that you are going to walk into that casino and gamble it away?"

Well the man replied, "No sir ... I have money for gambling."

我 有 钱

我在拉斯韦加斯时，一个男人走到我跟前说："先生，你能给我 20 块钱吗，我妻子要做手术，需要 1 000 元。我现在有 980 元了，还缺 20 元。"

我想了想问他："我怎么知道你不会拿着这钱去赌场里挥霍掉呢?"

可这人答："不会的，先生……我有用来赌的钱。"

A Matter of Age

A wealthy eighty-four-year-old man married a gorgeous twenty-year-old woman.

His friends were very surprised.

"How did you persuade her to marry you?" they asked. "We know you're rich, but a girl so bright and young and beautiful."

"I fool her," he smiled and said. "I told her I was ninety-four!"

年龄的问题

一个富有的 84 岁的老头娶了一个 20 岁的漂亮姑娘。

他的朋友们都很吃惊。

"你到底是怎么让她嫁给你的?"他们问道,"我们知道你很富有,可是那个姑娘是如此的聪明、年轻而且漂亮。"

"我骗了她,"他笑着说,"我告诉她我已经 94 岁了!"

Too Many Debts

John was aggravated about his many debts.

"Henry," he confided to his best friend. "I can't sleep anymore because I am so worried about finances."

"Sorry, buddy," answered Henry, "but I can't help you in that department. You already owe me $800."

"I wasn't going to ask you again. Don't worry."

"I can't understand why you are in this situation. You have a good, steady job."

"I know, but I owe money to the food market, the department stores, the liquor store, the landlady and you."

太多债务

约翰被众多债务缠得焦头烂额。

"亨利,"他对自己最好的朋友倾诉说,"我为自己的财务状况焦虑得都睡不着觉了。"

"很抱歉,老伙计,"亨利答道,"在这个问题上我帮不上忙了,你还欠着我 800 块钱呢。"

"我不是又来找你借钱的,别担心。"

"我真不明白你怎么会把自己搞成这样。你的工作很不错,又稳定。"

"我也知道,不过我在食品店、商场、酒店都有欠账,我还欠房东太太,还有你的钱。"

钱 这 东 西

"Why don't you pay off one debt at a time?"

"I would if I could, but if I don't have some money by tomorrow — I'll really be in a big jam."

"You owe the government back taxes?"

"No, I don't have enough money to bet on the horse races tomorrow."

"你为什么不一次付清一笔债务?"

"我能的话一定会的,不过明天我要是没有点儿钱的话,我可就要有大麻烦了。"

"你欠政府税款吗?"

"不是的,是明天我没有足够的钱赌马了。"

☆ **aggravate** /ˈægrəveɪt/ *v.* 激怒,使恼火

☆ **confide** /kənˈfaɪd/ *v.* 吐露(秘密等);托付

钱 这 东 西

Yesterday's Bread

Johnny walked into a bakery and handed the baker a quarter.

Johnny: A white loaf, please.

Baker: It's fifty cents now, boy. Bread's risen in price.

Johnny: When?

Baker: This morning.

Johnny: Well, all right, just give me one of yesterday's!

昨天的面包

约翰尼走进面包店，递给面包师一枚 25 分的硬币。

约翰尼：请给我一个白面包。

面包师：5 毛钱一个啦，小伙子。面包涨价了。

约翰尼：什么时候涨价的？

面包师：今天早上。

约翰尼：这样啊，那好吧，就给我拿一个昨天的面包吧！

Simple Life

James is an elderly tramp whose life is simple and uncomplicated. One day a wealthy gentleman found him asleep on his front lawn.

"Mister," the gentleman said. "This is my property."

"I'm sorry," apologized James. "I thought this was a park."

The gentleman looked sympathetically at the ragged tramp. "Mister, are you happy living this kind of life?"

"Sir, money and worldly goods do not make happiness," preached James. "To me happiness is the freedom to roam without the

简单的生活

詹姆斯是个老流浪汉，过着简单而常规的生活。一天，一位富有的绅士发现他睡在自家前院的草坪上。

"先生，"绅士说，"这里是我的地方。"

"对不起，"詹姆斯道歉说，"我还以为这儿是个公园呢。"

绅士同情地看着衣衫褴褛的流浪汉，说："先生，你觉得过着这样的生活幸福吗？"

"先生，金钱和那些世俗的东西并不能给人带来幸福，"詹姆斯喋喋不休地说，"对我来说，幸福就是不受社会、文化还有经济困扰地自由自在地漫

pressures of society, culture, and the economy. The sky is my roof and world is my bed. Give me all this, a piece of bread, a can of baked beans, and my happiness is complete."

"I admire your sincerity," said the gentleman and handed him a hundred dollar bill.

"Sir," commented James as he took the money, "you have made me very unhappy."

游。天空是我的房顶，大地就是我的床。给我一片面包、一罐烘豆，我的幸福就十全十美了。"

"我很赞赏你的真诚，"绅士说着递给他一张100美元的钞票。

"先生，"詹姆斯拿了钱说，"您让我很不幸福。"

☆ **tramp** /træmp/ *n.* 流浪汉

That Really Hurts

Mr. Jones undressed for the doctor's examination.

"I am going to press on various parts of your body," said the doctor. "Tell me if it hurts or not."

The doctor prodded until he found a sensitive spot.

"How long has it hurt you there?" inquired the doctor.

"Approximately three months, but it really doesn't hurt much."

"According to the X rays, lab reports, and my examination I think we'll have to operate."

那样真疼了

琼斯先生脱了衣服让医生检查。

"我会按压你的各个部位,"医生说,"哪里疼就告诉我。"

医生按了一遍,最后找到一处易痛部位。

"这里疼了多久了?"医生问道。

"大概有 3 个月了吧,不过真是疼得不厉害。"

"根据 X 光和实验室报告,还有我的检查,我认为你该做手术。"

"Oh, no!" moaned Mr. Jones.

"There's nothing to worry about," declared the doctor. "With our modern anesthetics and know-how, it won't hurt a bit."

"How much will the operation cost?"

"With the hospitalization and my fee, about thirty hundred dollars."

Mr. Jones groaned, "Now, that really hurts!"

"天哪，不要吧。"琼斯先生呻吟着说。

"没什么好担心的，"医生说，"我们有最先进的麻醉术和手术技能，你一点儿都不会感觉到疼的。"

"这个手术要多少钱？"

"住院费加我的手术费，大概 3 000 美元吧。"

琼斯先生抱怨道："现在真的疼了！"

☆ **prod** /prɒd/ *v.* （用手指、棍棒等）刺，戳

☆ **moan** /məʊn/ *v.* 呻吟；抱怨

☆ **anesthetics** /ˌænɪsˈθetɪks/ *n.* 【医】麻醉学

☆ **know-how** /ˈnəʊhaʊ/ *n.* 技术；技能

☆ **groan** /grəʊn/ *v.* 呻吟；用哼哼声表示（非议、烦恼等）

钱 这 东 西

Family Finances

A couple was having a discussion about family finances.

Finally the husband exploded, "If it weren't for my money, the house wouldn't be here!"

The wife replied, "My dear, if it weren't for your money I wouldn't be here."

家庭财务状况

一对夫妻在讨论家庭的财务状况。

最后，丈夫终于忍不住说："要不是我的钱，我们都没房子住！"

妻子答道："亲爱的，要不是你的钱，你还娶不到我。"

钱 这 东 西

A Letter from Mom

Dear Son,

I'm writing this slow 'cause I know you can't read fast. We don't live where we did when you first left. Your Dad read in the paper that most accidents happen within 20 miles of home, so we moved. I won't be able to send you the address as the last family here took the numbers with them for their next house, so they wouldn't have to change their address. This place has a washing machine. The first day I put four shirts in, pulled the chain, and I haven't seen 'em since. It only rained twice this week, three days the first time and four days this time. The coat you wanted me to send you, your Aunt Susan said it would be a little too heavy to send in the

妈妈写来的信

亲爱的儿子，

　　我这么慢才写信给你是因为是知道你也读不快。我们不住在你第一次离开时的地方了。你爸爸从报纸上读到一篇报道说大多数事故都是发生在家周围方圆 20 英里的范围内，所以我们搬家了。我不能告诉你地址，因为原来住在这里的那家人为了不改变地址而把门牌号带走了。这地方有台洗衣机，第一天我放了四件衬衣进去，开动机器，我就再没见过我的衬衣了。这个星期只下了两次雨，第一次下了三天，第二次下了四天。至于你想让我寄给你的那件大衣，你的苏珊姨妈说上面的扣子太重了，不好邮寄，所以我把扣子都剪下来放在了大衣

169

mail with the heavy buttons, so we cut them off and put them in the pockets. About your sister, she had a baby this morning. I haven't found out whether it's a girl or a boy, so I don't know if you are an Aunt or and Uncle. Not much more news this time, write soon.

Love, Mom

P. S. Was going to send you money, but the envelope was already sealed.

兜里。至于你的妹妹，她今天早上生了个小孩，我们还不知道是男孩还是女孩，所以我还不清楚你会做阿姨还是叔叔。没有更多的新消息了，以后再写。

爱你的，妈妈

又及：想给你寄钱来着，可是信封已经封死了。

钱 这 东 西

Tax Collector

Little Johnny was playing with his father's wallet when he accidentally swallowed a quarter. He went crying to him mom, choking on the quarter.

They took him to a doctor, who said that the quarter was impossible to remove without surgery. They consulted a specialist who was of the same opinion.

Then came a man who said he could get the money out in a jiffy.

He turned little Johnny upside down and patted him with great precision on the back of neck and, sure enough, the quarter rolled out.

Everyone was amazed, the father said, "You must be an expert!"

The man replied, "No, sir. I'm just a tax collector."

收税员

小约翰尼在玩爸爸的钱包时，不小心吞下了一枚 25 分硬币。硬币卡在嗓子里，他哭着跑去找妈妈。

爸爸妈妈带他去看医生，医生说只能做手术取出来。他们又咨询了一位专家，专家也说没别的办法。

然后又来了一个人说他能马上就把钱取出来。

他把小约翰尼头朝下拎起来，精确无误地在他的后脖子上拍了拍，那枚硬币就真的掉出来了。

每个人都很吃惊，爸爸说："你一定是个专家！"

那人答道："我不是的，先生。我只是个收税员。"

☆ **precision** /prɪˈsɪʒən/ *n.* 精确性；严谨

173

钱 这 东 西

Your Rubber Band

A man stood up in a crowded restaurant and said, "Anybody who lost a roll of twenty dollar bills with a rubber band round them?"

There was a rush of people claiming to be the loser. The first to arrive was an old hobo.

"Here you are," said the man, "I've found your rubber band!"

你的橡皮筋

一个人在一家人头攒动的餐厅里站起来问："谁丢了一沓用橡皮筋捆着的 20 美元钞票？"

一大堆人跑过来自称是失主。第一个跑过来的是一个老流浪汉。

"呐，给你，"那人说，"我捡到了你的橡皮筋！"

钱 这 东 西

The Bank

Banks will loan you money if you can prove you don't need it.

Bank accounts give a person a good feeling until they realize that banks are insured by an agency of a federal government that's over $2 trillion in debt.

Banks have a very interesting philosophy. You give them your money to keep — and if you try to borrow it back, they want to know if you're good for it!

I just went partners with my bank. They own half my car.

Even my bank doesn't have confidence in me. I have three things printed on my checks: my name, address and insufficient funds.

银　行

银行会贷款给你，如果你能证明你并不需要这笔钱。

有银行账户会让人感觉良好，可等他们知道银行因为欠债 2 万亿而被联邦政府部门上了保险之后呢。

银行有一套有趣的哲学。你把你的钱放在他们那里保管，当你想借回时，他们却要你证明自己的资信！

我刚和我的银行合股，他们拥有我的车的一半产权。

我的银行都不信任我。我的支票上印了三样东西：我的姓名、我的地址和短缺资金。

钱 这 东 西

Banks are very much concerned with the best interest of the town. And they get it!

A bank is a dignified institution that was established for people to have a place to keep the government's money until tax time.

The first drive-in bank was established so that people could show their cars who really owned them.

Why are there bank robbers? Bank ads make it seem like it's easier to just walk in and get a loan.

I must have a dishonest face. The bank asks me for ID when I deposit money.

If bankers can count, how come they always have ten windows and two tellers?

A guy walked into a bank and said, "I want to open a joint account with somebody who has money."

银行非常在乎本城最好的利率，他们确实拿到了！

银行是个庄严的机构，它的设立是为了让人们能有地方在交税日前保存政府的钱。

第一家汽车（驶入）银行建立了，这样人们就能把他们的车展示给真正拥有它们的人了。

为什么会有人抢劫银行？银行的广告使他们觉得这样走进去就得到一笔贷款更容易些。

我一定长着一张不诚实的脸，不然为什么我去银行存钱时，他们还管我要身份证。

如果开银行的会数数，他们怎么能有 10 个窗口却总是只坐着两个出纳。

一个人走进银行说："我想和一个有钱的人开一个联合账户。"

Last week I got a $5000 home improvement loan from my bank. I'm sending the kids to college.

One bank opened a branch near a cemetery. In the window the president put a sign that read, "You can't take it with you when you go, but here's a chance to be near it."

I tried to open an account in the bank yesterday, but they turned me down.

Why?

I wanted to open a charge account!

钱 这 东 西

上星期我得到了 5 000 元的房贷，我要用这钱送孩子们上大学。

一家银行在公墓边开了个分行。他们的总裁在银行窗户上挂了一块广告牌，上面写着："你不能带着它走，但放在我们这里会让你离它近些。"

昨天我想在银行开个帐户，可他们拒绝了我。

为什么？

我想开个赊欠户。

外文出版社图书推荐

精品阅读

21世纪英语沙龙丛书（英汉对照）

生活小品文　　　西方风情录　　　名言荟萃
妙语拾趣　　　　笑话集锦　　　　寓言世界
名人掠影　　　　名人轶事

心灵阅读（英汉对照）

人生篇　　　励志篇　　　情感篇　　　生活篇
情操篇　　　道德篇　　　箴言篇

西方风情系列读本（英汉对照）

礼仪与风俗　　　节日与婚礼　　　饮食与生活
时尚与休闲

笑话集锦（英汉对照）

婚姻悟语　　　　校园逸事　　　　男人与女人
上班这件事　　　童言无忌　　　　动物趣闻
钱这东西

品读人生丛书（英汉对照）

关于爱：有爱走过
关于幸福：幸福的滋味
关于理想：梦开始的地方
关于成功：生命的辉煌
关于自信：相信你自己
关于处世：美丽心世界

精品教程

大学英语演讲教程

市场经济英语

经贸英译汉教程

国际商务合同起草与翻译

高级汉英口译教程

大学英语四级词汇与阅读自然通教程

大学英语六级词汇与阅读自然通教程

英语口语八步速通教程

功能语法教程

WBO 系统英语教程：国际音标与语音

WBO 系统英语教程：英语时态与语言基础

WBO 系统英语教程：语法与语用

WBO 系统英语教程：语句结构与语感（即将出版）

WBO 系统英语教程：语篇与思想表达（即将出版）

WBO 系统英语教程：语篇与文体（即将出版）

职业英语课堂

IT 与电信业技术人员应用美语口语

IT 与电信业技术人员应用美语写作

IT 与电信业营销人员应用美语口语

IT 与电信业营销人员应用美语写作

计算机大众应用美语口语

英语沟通技巧　　　　　　　面试英语

12 招英语行遍天下　　　　　秘书英语

英文书信轻松写　　　　　　现学现用商务英语

商业英文书信范例